CHEMICAL
WEDDING

THE COLORADO PRIZE
David Milofsky, Editor

1995   *Strike Anywhere,* by Dean Young
        selected by Charles Simic

1996   *Summer Mystagogia,* by Bruce Beasley
        selected by Charles Wright

1997   *The Thicket Daybreak,* by Catherine Webster
        selected by Jane Miller

1998   *Palma Cathedral,* by Michael White
        selected by Mark Strand

1999   *Popular Music,* by Stephen Burt
        selected by Jorie Graham

2000   *Design,* by Sally Keith
        selected by Allen Grossman

2001   *A Summer Evening,* by Geoffrey Nutter
        selected by Jorie Graham

2002   *Chemical Wedding,* by Robyn Ewing
        selected by Fanny Howe

C H E M I C A L
W E D D I N G

R O B Y N   E W I N G

Center *for* Literary Publishing
Fort Collins

Set in Copperplate and Garamond.
Printed in the United States of America
by Maple-Vail and Pinnacle Press.
Cover designed by Matt Williamson.

Library of Congress
Cataloging-in-Publication Data

Ewing, Robyn.
Chemical wedding : poems / by Robyn Ewing.
p. cm.
ISBN 1-885635-04-4 (alk. paper)
I. Title.
PS3605.W56 C48 2002
811′.6—dc21   2002011687

The following poems originally appeared in the specified journals: "Wishing
out of the Disappearing I Vanish," "Hot Thread Original Hiss," and "Sum
Our Only Blue" in *Colorado Review;* "Thank God He's a Country Boy
Passing Sky" in the *Washington Square Literary Review.*

The paper used in this book meets the minimum
requirements of the American National Standard
for Information Sciences-Permanence of Paper
for Printed Library Materials, ANSI Z39.48-1984.

1 2 3 4 5 06 05 04 03 02

CONTENTS

I thank my teachers.

I

WISHING OUT OF THE DISAPPEARING I VANISH

No longer wishing mystery I vanish
into things:
Crooked pockets leak bodymadness.
Pilots stall absolute.
Local rain splits sending slenders.
Floods:
Take me for transparent.
Or a wandering prince
dreaming in drums.
Of men: His florescing tongue on the skyjacked price of gas.
Our separate waiting.
His variable-pitch typewriter.
He says this.
Into this:
Horizon papers.
Stars puzzle at their multiplicity
into her sleep:
A history of heart yet little blood.
Horns hollow.
Possible wolf in the tail.
As well as wearing the chin bone of a frog around one's neck
is possibly this:
Dry and ground into a powder the liver of a black cat.
*Mix with tea and pour from a black teapot.**
Some try an ivy leaf between the breasts.
How then these things:
I dress, I shoe, I tear.
Once a year one
at a time
it was: a kind of love

* *Black Cat Love Potion* as prescribed by W. B. Yeats

I step into sky and its usual color of thin.
He props the bathroom window with my collected Yeats.
For he smokes.
And he says: In its making reside seven gods.
Rice, he means, in each grain of rice.
So he eats them all.
Yet he doesn't read.
But sees: Multiple mint spots flung to the bathroom mirror.
As it is before breakfast he wears no pants.
And says: I have allowed my toothbrush to express itself.
Since here I stand months prior.
I wipe free the mirror into which I cannot hear.
Into which I cannot hear the wild ordering of mint spots.
Months in making.
For not yet known: This is not the deranged king I would lure
        from his dark hiding place.
For he sees now.
With pants.
On a phone I am hours from the hearing of spots.
Hours from hearing he says: Removal of earth-old stones
        imprinted with early shells is a violation.
So from my pockets I return them.
I return them to a blackbent Illinois river.
In artificial lighting come natural settings.
Shadows working torn under only noon.
In my graveyard.
For an oak planted one hundred years prior planted too close uproots
        my old resting.
And on his hands I hear two silver rings.
Of water flown not mine.
And in mercury puddles broken by white-crossed rain is fire.
And in mercury puddles broken by white-crossed fire I hear hands.
Beautifully fingered.

HOT THREAD ORIGINAL HISS

Reluctant shadows pull
towered
      longs. How far born must I go?
      sun asks
      moon asks
me   :This
most sad asking: What sorry can I
      to sun's unblinking
      moon's struck
eye   burning?
      — I consult
the polygonal jaws of our
small history. Erasmus says:
      I asking on
      my own head
bring moon for Look:
      Stars stay
pinned (it is
their un-
      cunning and)
of all things tropospheric
      I am   so
longwalked
spundizzy from
      excess of moon's
      naked size
bobbing
asks   my naked
      size: Am I too?
Wavelips
      strange   lapping
      moon's   absent
      rounds   lobbing to
ocean's unkissed
      lawn I

```
        send sun:
        to cool her cheek
        rest her table's
turning: She says:
        Back I must—I only know location
in her unlocatable
hotspit
        showers :and We
are quiet
together.
        Stars bell
                comes loose:
        her face flies—requesting I
sew her eyepockets:
        Tired she is
        of unfocus
far glummed
to slung black I
we      :come crackling
        in travel of (Original
        Hiss)
our swimtrails
        (eyeless calligraphies)
        ruby-born stockings
born in
        a needle a
        hot thread
hot born
born to :thread
```

BUILT SHE IN TWO DOLLAR WEDDING DO VOW

She grew up grown: built with old bricks and (no) fancy
        detail: to stand in a city of one: see here (there
was no father) other: windows up day all night:
        (some take note of this) for later: (anyone) can
climb in: some circle her cement skirt: some look up: to
        weather (inside) a sister in her basement
making messes (she can't get to it) is a brother on her
        seventh floor sets off pranky bombs: homemade:
and oh: up there: a mother leaps from the woman in
        her: from her roof past her windows windows
open to the falling several times a day it: the falling
        takes eleven years: (some) days she looks
otherwhere: across a river to split-level homes built to
        dream of when not standing: of futures as Dollar
Store parking lots and of once: up and down and up
        her stairwells cats a dog ran: (she protected
them) (a knight but smaller) (armor plastic): and they'd
        wander off: because (they do) and: some (do)
return (furry pirates) an (eye out) an (ear torn) with
        scrawny chests filled large with battle blocks
away: and of it: bricks that built her: (have small idea):
        here's a (day one) day: she bricks over windows:
so no one (even thinks) of coming: oh but: sun plays
        meddling hardball: wanting in: stopping to hover
to weigh assess odds for access then grazing on down
        a shadowy block (until: aha!) a shade is up! left so:
(a mistake) or (is it) sun: circles back enters stretches scats
        helling wood: a floor caught lazing its plumped
grains hugged tight to glossy scream: does she notice:
        built too lasting to indulge (luxury of): of collapse:
for standing is what she is: is built to: what: it is she:
        she says what: I: I do

Not signs of the zodiac; he guesses blood types.
She hears:
   You are an A.
   No a B.
He settles on B.
   B negative.
You are a monkey, she says— I, a rat.
Say place mats at Hunan Fat:
   Monkeys and rats mingle for life; though once
from a car moving, Rat threw the violently shiny shoes
   Monkey had bought her
   into noon's way of light.

Truth is old.

You: a notion, she says: Warm, but willed:
   By eye it's a moon on its hump of bowl.
   By eye it's sun eating sun.
Eye making what is:
   A navy of cats. On songback.
   A house on no land is not a floating house.
   Looking, making, wallpapering go on there
under:
   Briefly. Sky silver-boiled.
   Made only
so: in seeing

GREEN BLOTTERING WINTERING DISAPPEARING

It's those general questions (that want specific answers)
That muck the lattice. Such as:

How are you?

Since—I don't know.
    (Not since beginning to think twice of hanging upside down
from monkey bars playing dead playing blind observing light blottering
through woven color of the kettle cloth jumper up over my head).
    And so.

Here we are.

And so what of specific questions that demand a specific answer.
    Such as:

What color are your shoes?

(With eight preestablished choices on a color wheel this one's easy)

        Answer: GREEN

        —!However!—

Say the green is the green light makes when on your side back to window
first eye to me opening a morning pounding through blinds admixing the
milk white blue igniting iris making the green a winter grass green the green
of those grasses divided by violet ochre stretches of infolding hills slipping
down oceanside passes after a fall of only some rain particular to Highway 1
shot through with lacy sulfurs much like those shy-headed weeds name
unknown that hang in drawn-down arcs disappearing to low late wintering
sun when approached on foot around hilling bends in lower is it eastern?
Tennessee—

PAINTED AND IF SHE SO BLOOMS TWIN WILD PEARL

Painted lovers not of earth and dirt
    float: her ankles
    dangle: her scarf a bent horn: a dimension
    of two above a town of tiny wheat-puffed houses:
a man-form is the locked river at her back: twin hammocks
    pinned: a canvas to lake for sky: her view: down and
    beyond a hilltop of wild
blooming: his to specifics outside the frame: their faces of color
    collide: chromium yellow accidents: sap green where red
madder should be: cobalt
slung in a moping tree and out of this
    she dreams—

toes heels to earth: a march through chops of warm blue mud
baked up by quick spring:
    of a bed on a floor in a square house with a room to walk into
and maybe another: of a sock of pennies
    dropped down the throat of a metal stairwell and hands
run through cold and hot water while an imperfect
    meal cooks is: a map
    knit from her voice:
    its shower of pearl traveled
unraveling and if she so wants:
    to begin it all: again

Raft Now Sees Elsewhere Declaring Ears

It is a raft launched to a preoccupied sea built
        for her by him though once his feet loved hers
on land in a bed in a house on oak stilts by a highway. Out to
        this float he paddles without regularity it is
whenever he wants but this coming is becoming less and
        less. A habit winding down.

In conspiracy is the tide that now sees it a silly
        convention to come in go out come in go out (now
only out). From her float, she looks to moon who
        pretends to hear a noise from elsewhere so
gazes off in absent whistling (not very well).

About twice a week the man views his lover
        through a telescope. She is asleep or her head
is in her hands. He notes that she is the size of a broken
        pencil point.

One day he calls out through a bullhorn declaring:
        Somehow (as if this is good news for both of them)
we'll be involved forever! Words skipbump the roily seatop smack
        her ears and knock her into coldstung black.

Down she plumbs (a single petalwing) beyond light
        to a single bed of sea tin. Here she lies flanked
with years of stretch, a long pull down the bed's
        middle. Her fists are balled novas under her chin.
She is asleep. (When her eyes are not).

Pacing shore is the man. He skips stones without
        success. He urinates his name in sand with rococo
loopings: not concerned his lover-speck is out of view:
        still of this thinking that things thought: remain

MAN CALLED STILL SPINNING

A day when Man Called left
the room—plates still spinning on

his dreamsticks his air over-
perfumed with his verbal parquetry

when it all came down—shards
hyena-jigging jumping front to back her

bean-sized will not able to
convince her maladroit hands to

patroon it all back—face
and ears hushing alizarin in wait for

a morning glory ladder to
away her from knee-deep in baby

teeth plucked one-by-one so
soon so weaving her own aegis basting-

stitched with what's found—
tin-can lids and dime-store kite string

SPEED OF RED LIGHT AND DOG BREATHING FREE

In bed sitting up. Between dreams early A.M. A witching
        chin of florescence from an apartment hallway
sharply through slit-cracks framing a steel door streaked of
        paint from a previous decade the color of teeth in a
skull long buried (not in a coffin). Her head feels small
        in her hands, though it weighs as much as a
bowling ball. She recalls this from fourth-grade science
        when seeming unlikes first collided on a wall:
an illustrated chart of monkey to man and a poster of
        a single drop of rain plunging to mud magnified
millions: its catastrophe in a teary ring moving upward
        suspended: *This is how erosion begins,* said Mr. Coe,
though none believed a scrawny raindrop could do such
        destruction though in fourth grade all destruction was
enormous and what kept her from sleep was the ordinary
        horror of a social studies filmstrip of mud slides
so fast there is no time to run from house or car and the graceful
        noses of bombs easing from bellies of fighter planes
their quiet plumages up from earth a Bushman of the Kalahari
        standing smiling to thighs in the carcass of a slaughtered
giraffe his shins in blood and its drinking on his chin after
        a chase for days felling it with poison-tipped arrows
and her never quite believing that blue light, green light and
        red light all travel at 186,000 miles per second since
red is fastest since hottest and therefore angrier and anger is
        quicker and his finger, *That's inertia,* said Mr. Coe, indicating
to a quavery dome of water arched impossibly above the rim
        of a plastic cup that she believed (since it was
easier to) though inertia is still a mystery twenty years later and she
        waits only for sleep if it comes at all and for the next
dream to have its way and be gone: this dream of a pocket-sized
        dog a mutt held too tightly between cupped palms
of a man and its fur wet with sweat and it sucks milk from a flexible
        straw drinking down hard not stopping to breathe and
Aha! she thinks: *Ordinary dogs can drink and breathe at once!* and awake
        to relief now to small belief, winged.

View Enters Woman Only Absence

(I am not dreaming)
                    glittering misfortune's
                    tilt-yard logic
a nutshell halved gutted hard clean where
            living we curl
coupling our backs learning here is absence
                    my head sleeping in mice
nest in walls
            prayer in odd places
lawn's a slant decanting is
                    earth we are given—

                    in a basement (I am dreaming)
sealed in a tower of a city bridge missing stair
            window door
                    floor sandy enters
                    a woman
sweeping laughing her broom tip taps ceiling
                    tap tap tap (teeth
            lined in elbows of gold her
tongue licks them) *Lady*
            she says *Only way out is*
                    laughing tap tap
(nub of broom tapping) ceiling
            Lady only way out is—tap tap tap—*up*

Womanmade Twilight Drinks Her Anteloping
Lack of Edens

Recent century.
Noon.
Female backs car from drive to pick up organic milk and a few brave men.
It should take an hour.

13 years later.
3 p.m.
She's back with the milk and not brave men but a backseat of admixture men.
They elbow tease tickle fatigue the electric windows.

5:13 p.m.
Any day.
Backyard.
Female unsnaps and removes her tongue and hangs it to sun-sere.
Afterwhich it is Tupperwared and stored in the sideboard.

5:26 p.m.
Same day.
Backyard.
She stitches over her voice box with anteloping X's.
Overspent on lack of use.

5:27 p.m.
Same[2].
Her heart scissorwalks out her back from between her shoulder blades.
(She had policed it only from the front.)

5:28 p.m.
Same[3].
Around the yard her legs move to a biologic.
Without her.

5:29 p.m.
Same[4].
Her spine self-evicts.
(Spine's hollow replaced with a pint of artificially sweetened edens.)

5:30 p.m.
Same⁵.
A breast removed is dried for a doily and barked out is her sex.
(A last conflume.)

Twilight.
Night dines on sun's boneless remains.
She convinces the pool into a merry cocktail.
(Though it does not drink.)

Night night.
She performs a dive.
(It is remarked: *What perfect toe points.*)
Into unpetaled lips broken of sapphire.
(Where she tucks sky to keep it from drinking her.)

I will paint a yellow painting! A still life. But nothing will be alive nor
        sitting and it will be about shape shapes in love shapes not
speaking shapes standing waiting for a bus but there will be no bus.
        And once done it won't be for how it is will continue on its own
my back to it while I do things at my desk and it will hang above a
        bed in my skinny room and I may say *Hello Yellow Painting!*
Particularly when I'm home from days that want to take me off my
        bones and call my name and disappear. Days like those. And
Yellow Painting will calm us. This one room and I. And it will host
        surprises predictable like the great aunt who forgets the
buttermints in a tin in the sideboard and asks *How in the world did they
        get there?* and it was this surprise every week to her house for
Friday night dinner before Yellow Painting will be begun. If so. So.
        Others before you I haven't wanted and this not wanting
happens quick. A moment after the last stroke is struck and out you go
        for adoption. Like those of you in a basement in another state.
Since there is no room here. And all those painted faces to a wall in
        lightlessness until someone comes looking for a hammer or a
suitcase. Elsewhere you are on walls at the house of a man tired of
        house plants who wanted *some decorations.* And for when
I had space for complications of paint. So. If I start you and
        your one color Yellow Painting I may not take you from my
hands. Finish you. For I don't always pay attention to the end. And
        for this I. I apologize in advance if never we

SWUM SAWN FILLS PAPER FEET

Under her feet
a god rows
      terrible globes
swims
into where she's sawn she
      hands him her
casually
sun lengthens her bones his
      portrait fills her
walking profiles
      less roofed her paper
metal
reflection is a diving ache
      in floors lost in high-polish
a kitchen floor warps a moon
losing hoop
winnowing on wavy
wing born
      dark is how things
come born
so sawn

TELL the nun to shut up and mail you the box of money.
      Any order will do. STEAL a baby from the beach.
Pick a busy weekend for good selection. STAND akimbo on your
      front lawn breathing quick and hard and noisy
through your nostrils following your neighbor with only
      your eyes opened wide so the whites show all
around and stare like ice as he walks to his car. *Don't forget*
      the breathing. TAXIDERMY a dead pet. Do so only if
the occasion arises, into a turban-shape. Wear it to the movies.
      Sit in front. DRIVE slowly by Big City Appliance
on Beverly Boulevard where illegal men, sun-carameled, eyes
      hot and sharp into traffic, look for work. Waste no time
with hello. Ask frantically for six large men who can knit: *Knit fast.*
      ENCLOSE in the return envelope a dollop of litter-
encrusted cat feces for the violation of parking in front of a broken
      fire hydrant. *You may need an extra stamp.* FLY
screaming from your house wearing only a crucifix, home-made,
      the size of a sheet cake, waving a broom, a hankie
attached to its tip, like a surrender flag, in glory, up over your
      head, toward anyone walking his dog. *See Eugene*
Delacroix's 'Liberty Leading the People' for histrionical reference.
      BREAK INTO the junior high wood shop Sunday
morning and on the table saw cut in half your family's
      good shoes, long-wise, like melon slices.
Return the pieces to their closets before church or, if not church,
      the International House of Pancakes. CALL the wife
of the man you love and offer 3,500 dollars cash for her husband
      or a possible time-share arrangement. *If she is less than*
amenable, have baked and ready for shipping an exploding earthworm
      casserole. Get the zip code correct. PAINT your finger
and toenails with Liquid Paper®. Paint the dial of your watch
      with Liquid Paper®. In your garage create a shrine
to Mike Nesmith's mother, the secretary-inventor of Liquid Paper®.
      Tip: When the little brush inside the cap gobs up, soak it in
a medium-grade vodka. START a conversation with a brilliant
      genius. *In an area where you know exactly nothing.*
URINATE anywhere but the bathroom and feel. *Preferably better.*

To Word and Moon Sun Jackslips

A toward of arrows
        I travel and fast
untoward horizon's scoliotic is

how you hold my flight
               I (ore of yours ?) plan

inescape
        my prolific blindness

rootwanders
        to crows
        roads float in desert
I stand perpendicular
        moon slips
        sun jacks easy: if

                b). mud
     then   a). rain

words say so
words say sun is

        a coiled tower : marigolded
        a yellow rose-tipped oar : laking
        a cycloptic scream
for what word is say (?) I

redder   am redder

unsung say
        only asking

42nd Street and Eighth Avenue and a shy rain. A clerk no
      shoes in the window display of *Fun Emporium*
adds a few more rubber turds to the pile toppling from
      the bowl of a plastic toilet amid all standard
rubber jokeware: vomit in two sizes stapled to thin gray
      shirt board with those foam chunks suggestive of
the undigested noodle dinner, masks with eyeballs
      hanging by their sinews, truncated feet with bone
parts jutting like snapped twigs colored and splintered like
      hard white taffy made by great Aunt Catharine that
splintered in our mouths back when my brother and I
      snuck fake turds onto Mom's new rug at the top of
the landing then crouched behind the couch whispering hard
      elbows poking ribs, *shut up she's coming,* the wait
for her basement ascent with laundry or frozen meat and one
      more thing to send her wild, like she did, a stallion
broken, *Damn that dog! That damn dog!* Pranking our way
      through preadolescence with the whoopie cushion
on Mom's bridge night positioned under the wingback's
      seat (with a lot of pre-testing) then to our vigil on
the steps eyes waiting on a few hours of 'That Girl' hairdos
      on heads of neighborhood mothers tipping back
foamy-topped whiskey sours gondola'd down throats and
      smoke slow-hanging, back when all the moms
smoked, jokes we don't get, hoping our victim will be that
      Mrs. Argo, that violet velvet eye patch, since she
yells at us on our way to the tracks cutting through her yard
      we go to shoot things like cans and shoes and junk
found in the cattails when I had a brother who taught me
      things—like how to make bombs with saltpeter
zinc and sulfur and how to detonate a jeep of G. I. Joes
      duct-taped to seats with a Barbie across the hood,
Barbies whose hair I had cut, sent together with a shove
      over a hill, a bucket of water to put them out, then
the prank of faking death with ketchup squirts across our
      chests sure to wear a white T-shirt for maximum contrast,

lying by the curb for the mailman or for neighborhood dads driving
        home from Philly and Boeing or Scott Paper comes: Rain:

More determined now, beats me back to where I stand
outside and cold on Eighth Avenue forcing its life on me comes
        a manila-haired woman in a tube top worn as a skirt
stretched across ship-width hips legs in white Puss 'n Boots boots,
        one missing a heel. To a man in a cowboy hat with silver conchas
she states the terms: *Twenty for the room, twenty for me*, her eyes
        dull shields and he wants a better deal and huffs away
and returns with a new question: *Where can I get some hair dye?*
        His brown sugar finger is a cinnamon swirl above his head.
She points toward Broadway: *Cosmetics Plus, but you can't afford it*
        and to show her he can afford it chucks coins hard to street
while at work still is the clerk at his art of window display unpacking
        things in baggies, corks called *Fart Plugs*, and behind him
a wall of knives flanking rows of how-to manuals, basement-
        presses, in plastic wrap: *Hunting Humans, Twenty-One
Techniques of Silent Killing, Tactical Handcuffing, Successful Armed Robbery,
        Cheating at Cards, How to Make Disposable Silencers,
Lip Reading Made Easy, Defeat Industrial Spies, Weapons at Hand,
        Low Blows, Construction of Steel Hiding Places, The Art of Death,
Getting Even I & II, Revengeville, How to Get Anything on Anybody,
        Slash and Thrust, How to Start Your Own Country* are a few
and I follow inside a man, cheeks gravelled, a pinkie finger
        missing and I hide behind the *Sex Me Down* T-shirts and
he's in line to buy *How to Smuggle Anything* and asks grinny why
        Curious Punishments is on sale half-price and together
we hear: *Some of the techniques in there—they don't work so well.*

MEN COMING

      In head's house
Eyes: decoding :
      (men
coming)

Heat:
      (not
impact)
cause of

      extinction

Earth drowns
      her life
in nature's
wet vined
      crawling:

Every fifth thing alive is
a beetle—
      mountains
(attempt
      escape)
nippling to clouds
and moons (Pluto
almost got
      away) and on

Carries earth's
      (unswallowed)
rounds bladdersacks
of lazing
      oceans:
Nature's uninvited
      perhaps men
(coming) is

                    a mistake

Earth is

            (to be)
meant to be
unobserved
            is sun's

Self-sterilization
            (heat
eats) water
            men
come from
we come from
            (see : the five-fingered)
            tree shrew) to
when—

Fingers less
and less necessary
            eyes too
            soon (none)
done decoding
see: are we
a last gentle

            Meal
to be we are
(what went)
(will be)
            of sun

II

2 A.M. Woman Enters Boy Room Bar and Pays

Five dollars and inside it's a timber of lemonade light that cuts
        smoke and dark coning on a platform a go-go guy—
his ass muscles lift and flutter at odds, genitals fishflopping
        in a gathering of black silk whetting the room to
Diana is Supreme on TV screens five across and high with
        all her life to live and all her love to give sung to
her in whoops and squeals are paired seisms omnimoving in
        a crank and jerk crank and jerk cam: the room an
accelerator nailed blind to floorboards aviating and comes
        circling: the glycerined man with two-dollar drinks of
clear pink fluid from an unlabeled bottle with shot glasses
        in leather loops bandit style criss-crossing his
cartoon-hero torso: this job from an ad requesting *actor*
        needed and *must power lift* and ads ask the same of
slips of men with boy-featured faces behind the bar serving
        costumed shirtless and jeans low on hipless frames
performing placid dives of longing are abdomens into
        belts selling drinks with arms godgolden arms
designed to take her order of Amaretto and orange and
        carry her from the typical apocalypses the cement
hail and buildings bending and raining glass on heads in
        heads over and away to fleece hills are pine needle
beds made-ready by long-lashed evergreens who knew of
        her coming before they were seeds before she was
where she rests in the godgold arms his eyes petalling
        hers—until: *Your change ma'am* a hard shout
from boyface mouth his arms ending in hands made for taking
        giving bills and pouring drinks and behind her
on a wall are men on men in pairs pressing their body lengths:
        two in baseball hats spun backward to facilitate
mouth on mouth siphoning taking whole faces into dark
        cathedraling of palms with no talk with no
forething: a feeding exact so exacting.

The day John Denver died I cried, but not for him. All the
        crying? That was a coincidence. Meanwhile,
through the crying are shifty edges the collapsing world
        oozes into. Books levitate before me on a library
table. Buffalo tears plunk to lines of type doubling and
        tripling and lurching around and rising off the
page, shimmying to the right or left depending on which
        way the bellies of tears roll over the rounds of my
eyes to their bucket drops below. Some splotch over the
        black non-permanent pen of my notes causing red
and yellow and blue contingencies to run from one
        another as if suddenly repulsed or bewildered by
freedom, on the run in young panic, as maybe, a baby goat,
        one of an otherwise uneventful upbringing, after a
morning of tearing at grasses head to ground finding
        himself alone in a field of things too tall in a wind
waving with the shirk of a storm on rolling shoulders
        over the unsprouted wings of the tiny goat
shoulders. And just as sentences sentenced to page are
        heaped on and warped weak by flat pools, unable
to rise from knees, from the library's eighth-floor window,
        facing north, through the disintegrating elms and
the blur of runny-silver hot dog carts comes—an event—
        unexplained:

Something large and quick in the form of a seventy-five-
        foot-tall man, in overalls and those thick leather
gloves for mending barbed wire fences, a bit lost, maybe
        looking for the Port Authority and a bus to
Pennsylvania, taking Washington Square Park on the
        diagonal, over the chess players, his shadow-loom
rolling over rooks and backs and men playing who don't
        look up for anything and take it as a passing sky
mood, his legs over the Washington Square arch in a
        country stride, the back of his head disappearing
up Fifth Avenue and the day settling back to what it was

and will be and we studiers look up from our
books and out the windows then back to our books then
leaning a bit off our chairs to see what we saw,
curious as to where he ends up. We glance to one another
in fellowfeeling for an event not of this earth, not
of this time anyway, united out of our solitary study
shells, talk maybe later of the big farmer when at
five we descend with the elevator to the street when
I am done with the tears of a buffalo for now
suspended by the event of a seventy-five-foot-tall man on
his way to not being lost, not lost at all.

On Walk Jumps Sticky

sky's
thick cream

a motor boat's
low born engine

a squeal a small son
a man fishing

nylon arcs
fluorescent bobbers

a red life jacket

lake's greenglass
speaking in concentrics

limb's long bellies
skatterlinked

twistered butterflies
peddle my cheek

on groundweb's visibled plan
light in beads
of absent honey

underilluming leaf
a web's sticky thin

jumps a fish
a chip of pink

off from hearing
a lapping

lake's shiny flat patches
light's red roiling fingers

webs whirled flutes

and mud
cut with soles
of men and dogs

a tree of many breasts
sprouting fingersticks

roots unallow earth
its proper throat

old limbs fallen to x's, y's, v's:
several perfect crosses leaning

sun's noon is a faith
of butter

day's now gray wag
lake's silver-same sun's
silver-same

sky lifts
its lemon skirts

for rain

SYNCLINE SOME WIDTHIER CLIMBING

Heart's new oak dressed in old war
its repair of shoulders
      released
           some widthier than
a Susquehanna some
           a climbing rope sometimes
burning she climbs early
           spring's jointbent rain
collides of winters
           claim her back—its
lure—a nickel of sun a fix
           of blown deltas falling in dark
in twists of sun's lovely scientism

      splits
           her heart with plans
of drowning plots plot to set sun with
her fly-eyed fists
      for sun's accident of
           refusal
to stop knowing
      fingertree'd ribs
      not yours
      another's
for heart's
a random sun
      where fallen
      digs seed

There is no war so she will find one (driving) one eye on purpose
        closed, a pretend accident responsible for its loss.
Right eye tires quickly, disorientation, fatigue,
        light nausea, some fear (experiment abandoned
after four blocks) (rethinking) a phone message from
        the man who walked out when all was well.
Call if you need anything, is his voice. *I need not any but
        everything,* she says (west on Sunset) (decisions
beat) windows: *up/down?* air conditioning: *off/on?*
        when: *now/later?* Reports radio: *Yeast is a few
million years older than bacteria* positioning us closer
        in evolution to a cup of yogurt than she had
previously thought (blocks of car washes, lawns leaf-blown,
        franchises of cheap construction, glass, chrome,
cement) and out window she asks of L.A. (east on Olympic)
        Where oh where are the venerable? (to herself)
she points at Club Shackalack's marquee and says
        (to her newly made-up boyfriend) (the sort of
boyfriend who comes along just for the ride):
        Look, honey. Tonight Only, It's Manhole Snot.
They chortle together as they are soul mates (on lower
        La Brea) wherewhich she reinforces a driver's
faith in the random good waving a man in ahead of her
        to the Delicious Beef Bowl to (errand not necessary):
Ralph's: aisle 5 selling SOAP/BROOMS/MOPS/
        SHOES to (Budget Books) on intercom: *Help to
self-help, customer needs help in self-help. Help to self-help—*
        (returning to mail): one letter: *Dear Pool Owner*
and she crushes through petal-litter released enormous
        blooming purpled unshy like ten-year-old girls when
complete (and full) of voice before there is (a war to find)

ALIEN BREASTS IN EXAGGERATED PERFUME
FROM B.C. TO

VERY B.C.: Aliens speaking to a cave family:
(A cave family not yet clothed in sheens of polyethylycra)
We will return when you are dressed.

MATINEE: She dresses in Sunday dress on a Wednesday.
She fears a blow to the back of the head.
She moves to Row Last.

TUESDAY: A song drops its bells breaking its perfume.
Casualties: eighteen.

ON A BUS: A purse of our nation's foremen swing from copper beards.
And silver ponytails.
Profiles wince.

SEEN: Stars are a desert of clot.
Stars malign an earth only wanting:
A Good Night.

NIGHT: Man is up late.
To find the science.
To find the science in the short-pile fur nap on his cat's nose.
He weeps.

ALGEBRA I: Eighth-grade girl with breasts in bud.
She learns exaggerated respect.
She sits Row Front.

FUTURE: A sea blinks blank.
A sea folds neatly its rounds.
Her back is to it.

GIRL STILL PAPER BOY KITTENS SANITARY VIRGIN

Fourteen and his parents are away and you're wearing the lame bra the one missing a clasp since caught in a drain hole of the washing machine barrel so you wave away his offer of help in its removal and leave it on while he works his length working this funny chore over you that is new and you don't mind and his body convulses and is he sick? Will he vomit? And the poster of a Charlie's Angel in a red Corvette over the bed and a trophy of a football player missing a tarnished arm on a windowsill and he yells for Mary and God alternatively seven times then the warm wet deposit on your kneecap is mopped off with a tube sock and that was it? you ask only yourself driven home in the Mustang missing the front bumper because tomorrow there is a geometry test and by the Oompah coming from behind his door your brother has given up the viola for the sousaphone and your cat is again having kittens in your underwear drawer and your father is hiding in the basement to stiff again the paperboy knocking and knocking and three days later you confess to your mother since you have all the symptoms from the brochure procured from the nurse's office that you are irritable yes moody yes tired yes increased appetite yes yes yes and on the phone you hang up on the woman at the free clinic with questions you can't answer like when was the first day of your last cycle? since it never comes when it should still working itself out with the moon and your mother taking over like the army making a big deal of the trip to the hospital for her a day out of the house in pearls and pantyhose and shell-pink lipstick and shopping at Saks after the urine in a cup after the cold metal tongs pry you in two and after you sit up and off snap the doctor's rubber gloves and from the little sink his wiry white brow reading puzzle-ment and more questions that embarrass with words like ejaculate orgasm penetration and tired you say yes to it all not having any idea what and he leaves to confer with your mother you swinging your legs with the plastic uterus with removable parts on the aluminum rod stand and the illustrated chart of conception to delivery with em-bryo as peanut and your palms over your bowl of abdomen and what is in there and you want lunch and to lie down and a nurse leaves a sanitary napkin in the changing room telling you to dress and out of the parking lot it is a mother and her virgin hymen intact back to the suburbs told to put on her seat belt and take her feet off the dashboard wanting the name of the fool health teacher who she will call directly after the car lecture that informs you that sperm cannot impregnate from a deposit on a kneecap as it is Girl Still flipping down the vanity mirror for another application of Bonnie Bell Dr. Pepper lip gloss.

DOG FINDS CROW UNSERIOUS

Backyard Illinois.
A violent mangle
of black shine a chop of feather—
      a crow finds food a
      garden snake
southside a garage
where the landlord's
stepson refuses
      to mow
full of
renter's junk—
a bird's nest
      a scribble
      a hurricaned turban of
prairie grass a long
      language of kink
      from rafter
a roof allows
      broken sticks
      of white rain
stinging pits
of clear o's on
      mud floor
a square of carpet gone gray
      pink baked
      weathered out
a photograph of a boy diapered
      forehead
      run through
with a nail
      to a beam and
      a drawing—a snowman
      one crazy eye
scarf striped with all the crayons in the box
signed 'AMBER' backward 'R'
      belly of 'B'

a tire blown
a box marked 'Mary'
flipped and spilled
  old wallets
  no money

  a jockey statue
  cement face cracked black
at its boots
fenced for life
  poor
  unserious
a pair of dogs
  seven knocked-over
  buckets of food
sleeping days
  forehead to forehead
paws
a loving tangle
  square heads
full on blank dream

WHAT FINAL GOD DOG FOOD FEET DAMN BLESSING
Newport, Pennsylvania, on the Susquehanna River, October, 21st century, in One Act

A lot didn't go right but it didn't go that wrong either
      the day we buried God. TED, the man behind the
plexi at the Exxon knew something was up. That autumn
      leaves darkled straight to brown, avoiding
hues of embarrassment, aborting early to commingle
      grass somewhat rudely, some said.
ARRANGEMENTS. The final arrangements. There was
      some bickering as to God's feet. What final shoes?
The sensible or the fancy? It was left up to the desultory
      mortician, HAP SMILEY, tired of a life ordered
with death. He ordered: *God's damn casket will be closed!*
      WORDS. The final words. UNCLE JESS gave the
eulogy chosen unanimously for having worked at the Jet
      Propulsion Lab in Pasadena. Heard were the
standards. He didn't know the deceased all that well.
      *Uhmm. God? He was a good listener. Uhmmm. And
by no means easy. He practiced. That uhmmmmm. Uhm.
      That Whatchamacallit. Yeah. Tough love.* FOOD.
The Final Food. TED's sister GAIL from Crystal City,
      Virginia, was coordinator of the wake food to be
served in the church basement. But she forgot to assign a
      main course causing to show up: three Waldorf
salads and five dozen cupcakes, iced orange and black
      with pumpkin faces for Halloween. BLESSING.
The Final Blessing. With God gone, who would bless this
      food? UNCLE ALFIE, the town dyslexic, while
scribbling on a napkin, discovered that GOD rearranged
      is DOG. All agreed, DOG should bless this food.
Well. Not all the food was blessed, not the baked beans.
      BEANS. The Final Beans. AUNT SHIRLEY's polio,
assembling her asymmetrically shorter by 6" on her left
      side than her right, drove off with the baked bean
casserole, left above her eyeline, on the roof of the Falcon.
      Evidently she had no idea until the explosion of
Pyrex and beans in her rearview mirror while ambitioning
      a U-turn across the median of the Northeast

Extension. *She drives all cockimamy,* reported sister ETHYL,
who impaled an eye with a mascara wand when
Shirley's foot slipped off the block of oak nailed to the
accelerator pedal that makes her height legal for
driving, tossing the car forward. This was the assumed
cause for ETHYL, who owns the house they live
in, to raise the rent on SHIRLEY by $7.50 a month.
A SCUFFLE. The final scuffle. Some folding chairs
were overturned when CHRISTIAN, a career driver for
UPS, and NATHAN, an importer of hand-blown
Czechoslovakian glass beads, argued Ebonics, all blamed
on UNCLE SAMMY's spiking of the lemonade:
also cause for the act of the HUDSON TRIPLETS, who led
two dozen sheep from their parents' farm into the
church basement, sending the food table on end, causing
HAP's musically inclined son, LINCOLN, to slip
in Jell-O and fracture his wrist. His mother, MARGE,
wept the only tears of the funeral, her son's
career in marching band over for the season. BOB, a gifted
hygienist, was called upon to apply a compress.
That Bob. He has such a flair for compassion, cried MARGE,
kissing Bob on the palms. QUESTIONS. Some final
questions. On the way home, 2nd cousin CATHARINE
wondered to her legal secretary husband, GIL,
about God's will and testament, and heard back, *Was
none.* MAUREEN, a weight-lifting ice cream
scooper hitching a ride back to the city, lay across the
back seat, stockinged feet out the window, skirt
unzipped for too many cupcakes, and wondered aloud of
God's last words. *Were none,* she heard from Gil,
who knew sometimes what he knew. *Huh, just like that,* said
CATHARINE. *Oh, my stomach. Pull over! Pull over!
I'm going to launch,* moaned MAUREEN. GIL and
CATHARINE smoked by the car while MAUREEN
gagged up orange and black icing and a few candy corns.
A few miles later, a tire popped on a smeary patch

of caramel and broken glass that was AUNT SHIRLEY'S
      baked bean casserole. Gil fumed, Catharine sighed,
Maureen clucked. Each said nothing, thinking ahead to
      what will be the same old, same old of tomorrow.

HISTORY MET DRUNK OCEAN BITTER BABY DRUNK

(The quick road to breakfast was met with great opposition from a united sort of front. Lean beefs from out of everywhere living hoof to mouth took any work offered though so proud of neck. Saplings forgot. Willows slept for seasons and not from fatigue. Grass grew embarrassed. Uncontrollably, the sun began to wink. Oceans gave up. A crop of oranges refused to become just that and sat in purple boiled skins. Baby teeth stayed put. It was the year of everything at once: the year we spent at the bottom of the lake in a flip-top can. Until came a moment after a while. Oranges renamed themselves Violets. Mouths stayed small to house baby teeth and meals were drunk. Ocean stretched flat black and together swallowed the bitter ore named Sun. Used then were flashlights).

SUGAR SMASHING SLENDERS
RE-REVERSVING NEVER GARDEN

Downward slenders
soured open   water
garden gone   in it   sinking   runny a
florid-a of sugar   flung   gullied breast
bicuspids flown   Adam what's   in

your mouth   ? a curtain of   orbit   oh.

oh

earth

a hover twists

down to slenders   arms

her cross   crowned not   this sun re-re-
versing   fixity   smashing   quartzes
blanked open   there.   there

was   there   never   ? a you

a
spring—

MEANWHILE ON SEA UNHEARABLE

Bullnecking waves
                        trip   sound
of drums in earthless   drum
            a many-fisted god (mute weary)
punching cardboard
            waves   endknits of eyelets
                        petticoated fingers
a liquid mangle
            of confused bellies
                        arms over heads
mizzling back in greasy stretches
            low backs
            plattering
next coming—
            undisturbed :

            one-color rocks   chin-litter
hill's black
unfigured faces for
            topless clouds
            hum heavy on mean
            shoulders   grind east
smudging (easing?)
sharp smarts of broken
                        mountain crowns
heaven healed
            born torn

TICKLES RUSTY KNEES TOUCH

An ocean rolls
her rusty hips
            to pier
a slip of street cat (dynamite-
            stick body) presses
            to shadow beyond
                        a storm beats

today's bluing sill—
in red velour top
a sleeping mother's
                        sandy wings
            her small son
            a little lover (their
knees touch) clouds

                        bottomfeed mountain
brows   waves
            fan tongues
            feuds of white
collapsing (shore
            tickles last lips

                        unhearable)
face-down confessions
            bursting
            dime-sized rages

To Dream Your Oral Universe Diving Lie!

Dream! mad instructor! most lovely disease! actless play!
          not for us! false recipe! cosmic orphan! broken
          irons of a universe flown! expelled to so drown
          heads! living yourself alive! in our oral amnesia! a
          cry of night weddings! in skull cups in mornings!
          you scatter! for! do you sleep! by day by day
Thieving vocabularies! with animal industry! to moon's
          wobbly fist! we lie! drugged dollies! nocturnal
          invasion! this hemisphere! another! your skippity
          heels! on our respiration! nightwork you change!
My meaning! placelessly precise are you! or are you!
          another universe's dreammare! playmare!
          drowning stolen fluencies! or we are! one dream!
          nightly per galax! together writing to ends of
          diving! you! pilot-author! I surrender! erase
          open! to what will you! want me to see!
(Dream now)! Uncle Bob in Groucho Marx disguise leaves
          his job as bookkeep at Sun Oil to rally support
          from a backyard in a Mandarin-speaking
          Kentucky for national recognition of a new color:
PLUMQUAT!

MERCY SWIRL BELOW NECK THROWS PAPER DICE

THIRTEENTH MILLENIUM A.D., perhaps. The end of
thousands of years of struggle. Each soul considers
any other its equal. Each is secure. Mercy clangs
down from the stars. People swim with long
Olympian strokes in pools of pure cane sugar. It is
a world beyond the spank of law. Earth has
matured nicely into a nutty cherry nougat. Oceans,
rivers and seas lap and swirl thick with vanilla
macadamia milkshake. There is no need for
agriculture. Each carries a monogrammed pick axe
to chip nougat to eat and a double-wide straw to
drink from all that flows.

A THURSDAY NOONISH: A box of bricks falls from the
roof of Mercy Michael onto the head of Mercy Paul.
Mercy Paul was on his way to visit Mercy Marla
for nougat tartare. *I forgive you!* yells Mercy Paul.
He cannot feel his arms, his legs, anything below
his neck. Only his head is alive now. *I forgive you,*
yells Mercy Michael, *for walking under my falling
bricks!* Mercy Paul's limp body accepts the offer of
a ride to Mercy Marla's in Mercy Michael's
wheelbarrow. This becomes an errand delayed a
few years due to the need for Mercy Michael to,
first, clean his cluttered garage.

A SATURDAY DAWN: Gods Great And Not So Great
hang in the eaves of heaven. They throw dice.
They tell tales of the happy-bad old days—when
treated to the theater of struggle of unequal men
playing it all out before them and for them. Back
when raised faces asked for things. Back before
men knew that man-sized mercy works just
as well. Not helping the Gods Great And Not So
Great is their Saturday support group: 'Manless
Gods Who Mope.' Wailing notes not yet invented,
the Gods Great And Not So Great row off for
universes less solved.

SEEING I KNOW BECAUSE I HAVE SEEN IT LEFT BE

In heaven, or what have you, there is only swimming. Not swimsuit swimming but air is liquid and moves in gentle chops and in it you tread in what's not water and not for your life as there is no effort on your part and you're not actually in it as there is no in, no out. Its main feature is relief of effort and of divisions of things from, let's call it for now, quiet hell of even sleeping, and days that demand your definition from hard-edged verticals like a city of them or grasses or that one tree after fields of only none and unrealized is how hard on you is seeing. Days focus on this imposition of perpendiculars and on narratives on you over you, out, for example, car windows doing its telling from horizon's benign palm on which walking upright even in dreams is fixed, until. Into this gentle chop of clear and swim your eyes are relieved of the defining and say there is a figure seated, and his smile comes to you in buoyant shifts riding each chop in cropped leaps and an eye for a nose and an ear returns and from elsewhere in erasings, arrivings, leapings, not concerned with what was the necessity of it, it is you, left, left to be.

She asks. He says, *Shut up and tell me a joke,* then adjusts
his sun reflector, just so, under his chin. He orders an
angel to bring him another highball, his third since
creating a dozen new universes from a fling of toenail
clippings. She says, *It's all so easy for you.* He says,
You're boring me. Then he calls Tom Cruise for a spin in
his Formula One El Camino, the one with the ropy
chain of gold around the license plate.

A man walks by in an angel costume. He lugs a three-piece set
of powder blue American Tourister hardshell luggage.
She asks, *If you can't talk to him, then who can you
talk to?* The angelman answers, *Him? Grow up.*
Then he laughs so hard his cardboard wings ignite.
He boards a skybus packed with angelmen in swimsuits
carrying coolers and cheap beach chairs. She yells,
I hope you get feather rot! The skybus pulls away and
disappears into a hole in the mostly blue.

He is back, from Tom Cruise, adrenaline pumped. He says,
He's not what you'd think, in person, I mean, for an actor.
She asks, *Who?* Drunk, he shoots a few moons from
the sky with a slingshot. He aims too high and zings
a new universe. It collapses behind her. He says, *Oops!*
She feels the suck then the silence. She turns to ask:
Why did you do that? (This particular universe was
a baby, only three skillion years old). But, he's asleep,
snoring in mutters, slingshot hugged to his chest.
She steps to the edge of the gone-black where the
universe had been. She squints and sees no fire,
no flood, no frogging hail, no swarms of things.

She thinks, *That's funny.* He snores himself, and a few galaxies,
awake. He says, *What?* She doesn't answer and sits
cross-legged before the easy stretch of long newborn
calm, its deserted skirts, her heart's wild walking
having rowed past old edens no longer needing.

IDYLL GROWN BURNED WANTING

If your name I forget
          forgive it it is technical
it is my shoe walking I
          follow flower's hired faces
flock dots horrified
          of funerals we bring them
anyway we return grown
          bowbent I catch you
in your lap believing in
          again nature's inventions
in no error in the womb no
          prerequisite for a miracle
you are
so earth
          will inherit herself for is it
too wanting to live in her
          all at once from my
power of invisibility I ask
          whose future will I fake
in flowering I having burned
          through cremation this
flower and I walk face in hand
          it is my only walking

TRAVELOGUE #9-X: GLOSSY VACATION HERO MISSING!

I.

I greet the pixies at my delta.
We koo and hackle do the Ringadinga.
We tea!
We check into Vacancy Sparkling Clean Free HBO on Route 6 off I-80.
Minus specifics upturned are a few plastic ice buckets and some noses.
There is no concierge that we like on duty.
Into the deep end we!
Minus swimsuits left in our valises.
Fun without us!
Ice the size of rice floating in our Diet Squirts that we take for rice!
Art makes us cry: On Pay-Per-View it's a blind child, her profile a hero's.
A hero is always herself.
The many mountains in us!
We awake feeling not the many mountains in us but the worlds between them.
For who can marry a mountain?

II.

Off we.
To his desk of boxes.
Upon his desk of boxes in a double-wide trailer home facing Airport Road.
This is where he said he will.
And he is 82!
It will be a book he will write to prove the provability of the Bible.
A proof proving the proof of the Bible.
A proof proving the proof using no other source but the Bible-in-Itself!
And he is 82!
He'd better get started I said.
And I said: I is proof of I!
Off Airport Road.
Lies fly.
Good lies.
In other places.
We are.

III.
Superfresh.
Aisle 8: All known lengths of rice.
From aisle 13, we hear this, because he was so loud about it:
When I was a kid my watch would run backwards and stop.
And he was so loud about it.
A hike through man-made hunger.
At aisle's end.
A Free Sample Lady!
She coughs twice and polite into her rubber glove.
One for each of us.
One each for her too.
For she chews two!
For free.
We are!

IV.
We will return to find our garbage missing and there will be questions.
Are we famous?
Has someone gone through it?
We will return and on a glossy flier find a 60,000-dollar Starting Salary.
And a Company Car! Life and Major Medical! Dental and Disability!
And Ten Days Vacation!
Glossy and.
For the fee of.
Of free.
Free of!

Summer Glass Dashes Scraping Opposites

4 A.M. Cat licks electric outlet and lives. I consider dying my eyebrows to match my all. I tire of no belief in things. Note aversion: 1). xylophone. But love of: 2). square rooms. Know that 3). palliatives can be permanent (if kept up) is day. Woken of birds. First one then all going kerplooey to a light next door. Is his wife. Up and scraping carrots her eyes she presses with the backs of her hands over the kitchen sink and at opposite ends of the house. The man is up. And his hair. The color of those things that grow by the side of the road silent-headed in North Carolina. A platinum wheat that fuses in twilight hue for hue as to appear disappearing this man. He writes love letters—with many dashes—on the dashboard of his car to a papermaker he met teaching casting. That summer it was that summer. Of glass.

SUM OUR ONLY BLUE

Fingerflames
        lake-long
    a far boil across this
our only blue
redbed rivering
    above (becoming
see) below : soil's
torn fill
         however-entered
   seeds nosepoints
righted prayer-
heads huddle-
    bottomed
for when
for water
for will
        sun sleep ? what
mighty littles—
battled from
   seedcoat's open
      necks (temporary
oubliettes) to
bud to flower to
sum : endfruit :
      each : a truth
   of each multiplicative
inverses love
    crosses leaping
centers disinterest
free to from
care but immediate
      claim none (but
(mother for) each
is : other's
   mother for what
is (mother ? merely

perfect) endfruit is ;
is not flower is ; is
        not bud is ; is
        not seed is ; is not
end mother ? : end
        moves in these:
        reciprocal : equations
                a calling she calls
comes the absolute—
a floating erase : as
a wave : each is ; is
                not its last (end
and) so : end ; end-
        flower we are
and one : sum

SPRUNG FAULTY SILVERS ON WILD HEM

Night releases recitation of snow brung on spring's
        previous green
on remarked down daffodil caps (lumped
throats) and ice—
        evening's fluttery inks
        newly moon's cradleblade
sparkling sharp
        weakened thunder
blocky rain
cranked tumbles
dragged off for rain's steeper
        throats—pinch-slips unloosed
        on running heads on stung pavement
        garden's wild
winter-silver hay untucked
backsliding
wind (a chill choir) call lungs of sleepers
        sheets hung
for curtains belling night's
        faulty breath
        a negative flash spines open sky
claiming back
settling weathering
tailing hems east—sky's whole black
        set square
back to morning

Womanwho Visualizes Perfectly a Room
(She Has) Seen Not Before Today:
      Is the Age of Her Fatherwho:
      (That Once Instead):
      Coming (Not Home):
      A Stop: 'The Pines' for:
      A Drink. Subsequently to:
      This (Said) 'The Pines' for:
What Would Be the Next Number of (It Was) Years:
      Followed (Subsequently By):
      Forfeiture of Job:
      His Place in Bed (Beside His) (Then) Wife:
      The Girl (Woman(now)who):
Visualizes Perfectly a Room (Before):
      Earth Kissed (into Eyes) Bloom and Before:
      Moon Hung Its Face Out For Sale in:
      (A Room, i.e., Room 'A') that:
She Dreams Herself From:
      Comes: Inventory this Room (said): 'A':
      Missing:
            1). Floor;
            2). Ceiling;
            3). Walls;
            4). Egress;
            5). It Is:
(Thus Said) by Officials Officially Stating:
      We (Ahem) *Have Visualized Perfectly This:*
      (A Room, i.e., Room 'A'):
      Not Before Seen and (Herewith So Thusly):
      (Thensohither) Conclude:
There Is No Woman Everwho Was So (Everso) *Here:*
      (Ahem)

TRAVELOGUE #122-K: SHINY PHOTOGRAPH LEGS HER

Atlantic City. Someone's old aunt. Aunt Sissy. We went to visit. Before the casinos. On the bay side. But I wanted the beach. We were here for the beach. And the boardwalk. And to play Skee Ball. And to win those tickets that get you those prizes. There was her husband Moe in a plaid bathrobe he wore. All day. Helping her. Holding her by an elbow up from the side of the bed. She gets up slow and he is slow and finally they get her up. To her walker. And from the other room I see these chip things that make a circle around her feet. Like a pile of Frosted Flakes. Is she eating something in the bedroom? I am not allowed to eat in the bedroom. Old people must be allowed to eat in the bedroom. Then I see up close these things are coming off from her bloaty pink legs. Onto green shag carpet. Chips of skin. From off her legs. Legs that don't seem like real human legs anymore. I wander around. Waiting. And on the TV in the living room is a photograph of Aunt Sissy. *Miss Pennsylvania 1938.* Shining hair like a racehorse. Like a commercial for cream rinse. Her face skin is dark caramel with milk evenly mixed in. I ask if this is really her. I can't believe it's her. I sit on the couch. Waiting for the beach. I say I'm here. I'm here for the beach.

ABSTRACT MISSING ITS LOOKED UPON FIRE HIPS

A pigeon hops the curb and crosses
between the yellow lines and a black cow
her tongue a floppy continent
licks the face of her blonde calf sleeping under
moon's melon-sided
forehead when it was when he flew through my center and I
shoot now
at random targets and rivers test the cupping
of land's faith for what is nature's unavoidable bloom is
moon's crisp hips its undress of art is
coming a hillside a bruise of violets
drowning green fire a leaping in the profile
of a paper drinking cup
missing its tail but lime smoke over cranky cottons
thickly wandered for a teacup
less its saucering after the artist leans her brush
for lunch walks
a prickly cactus
drunk on liquid rust and comes
a pair of paper-white tongues
a Mourning Cloak butterfly
impossibly hinged

If you. When you get far enough out there. Time bends. Okay. So. This is a space talk and. Okay. So you've heard or overheard it. Before. Maybe. Says everyone's (got a) crazy uncle or so says. The genius of the century (same) so. It's a day. Average. Out there. This is space now. Where time. You got it. Bends. On let's say it's a Tuesday. For now. (This will change for Ever). Okay so. Here we are it's: a walk around the block. Up in space now (beyond it actually). And you are. Say the walk is: a neighborhood walk and ha! Coming round the cul-de-sac! You! Say hello to ha! (Not the ice cream man. Paper boy. A guy in space trunks watering his pachysandra). You say hello. To you! Yourself. (Stay with it.) Okay. Now then. You're thirsty from your little walk (and from all the Saltines) for (let's establish there are crackers in space). And so. You're inside your space house. And water from the tap takes off. Around the bowl of Space Duds (think Milk Duds minus the milk as there are no Guernseys to date in space) then zips. Out the front door and. It's headed for the neighbor's garage and. You run! And arrive! But the word *arrive* exists not in time to see water arc like a sickle into your glass in hand and. Oh ha! You look at your watch (minus hands) and it says two p.m. For three days. And. The hours of 7, 8, 9 blink by in a few nanosnaps (or not at all). And don't bother with January or May or any of the others and a Thursday means. Not one thing so. There is no knowing. Ha! So says. Law of the sublime: It's too big to! As are infolding silky heels. Of space. You. At first. May wonder. Where they make the crackers. And. Give up for why. In space. Since. In space. Every Where is at. So never are you. No where ha! Comfort is small but small is! Let's say. In space. This is!

I see you
don't.
I can
make you.
Fleas have
my cat.
In the
crazy
good.
Not god,
not now.
I am you.
I will fall
again.
Is this my
voice?
Art costs
too much.
I want
some
rules.
Do I see
you?
I learn to
seem.
No more
Good
Humor
man.
I am not

you.
I know I
forget.
I bring
you along.
No more
Dream
Team.
No one
should
die.
Child-
less
mother
of three.
His
vagina.
What if
it's me?
Go for the
money.
Lost, at
home.
You led
me here.
I lick
my cash.
This is my
voice.
Box-office

migraine.
No more
good
sports.
Lose a
loss, soon.
Tell me
it's me.
Shame-
shy,
desire-
free.
Duck-on-
a-Bike.
Spank the
distance.
I cart
my body.
Down
words,
behave!
Go solve
yourself.
His
primal
cream.
Original
swim.
Climb the
burning

sheet.
Clam-like
vigor.
That
contag-
ious
Horse-
Love.
Those
common
junky
birds.
Work-A-
Day,
Death-A-
Day.
Comes
calling
all wars.
Want
what
they
want.
Unfarmed
pockets.
Walk
housefly!
Carnival
lice, again.
Comb the

seems.
Pawn
broker-
priest.
I know no
one.
Take me,
so what.
Like it,
so
what.
'Miaow,'
you say,
'Miaow.'
I am
a man.
Jack-a-
ninny.
I meant
to fall.
My life
owns me.
Owes me.
The cat
speaks
daisy.
I know
you know.
Am I
driving?

Am I
driving?
People
help, I
forget.
Doggie
bags left
behind.
Love me
for my
money.
Do it
over
there.
You came
from me.
You
came
for me?
Clip 'n'
Save.
Utterly
smooth.
I'd rather
watch.
Feet
last.
Even
if it's
fake.

TAIL OF LACY FITS WAGS MY FLAT SLINK

Windows furred
    in flame in
inverted cathedrals your eyes are knowable
in only
    fragments: to be naked you request
    when cutting my hair
hair tips
of corn's
    October wag—
clouds nosing miraculous bouffants
of spiraling
hay my
    greeding eyes on wobbly parallelograms (little drunk
suns) march your shoulder sleeping—
    my flat heart
    its tail of slink
(once quick) lit runs
swept of
walled fire
feeds (to own) extravagant
    lacy fits (cuffs blooming
broken
waking)
    shaken of red

Coney Island August. Behind ruby velvet curtains blotched the color of tongue. For two dollars it is up steps of white paint crackling like glass to see *The World's Tiniest Woman.* Sitting for she cannot stand. In a square crib of unpainted ply. Her dress pressed white the size of a fancy dinner napkin. Her head an adult's. And legs lumps of inarticulate fists. It is hot. With a tear of cardboard from a box of *Trix* she fans herself. And at the exit is a red plastic bowl with a 'Hello' markered on its side. Its contents: a dollar bill and a dime and now a dollar more. And to her: *You must be hot.* And of water offered a shy smile says in its not saying. No. No. No.

Refusing flight
    dirty broken birds
    go ungroomed
forego garrulity
hobbleskirting throats
    try on smiles
markered on paper cups
attached with rubber bands
    two for forty-nine cents and some
are delighted, some think:
Gardyloo! and some
    want their money back and there is
some violence and produced
is a roscoe and some garboil
    and a few beaks
    become missing
dragged to lung fields
for bundling
    plumbering slinging
knocked to before
    memory
before first milk

TRAVELOGUE #9-V: I-80 AMOCO RUBIES BURNING INK

Three miles from GAS. And white arrow. Early August Amoco. Six boys. Two on bikes. A stone (toppled). Turns taken. Kicked: an R.C. machine. Its forehead (meekly pinking). In flank stand doors (broken guards): 'MEN' and 'WOM N'. (No 'E'). Sticky puddle. Flies black a dizzy knotting. Heat a smack. Horizon sags hollow. Jet stream (losing starch) (not direction). Boys see (in a cough of) lesser weeds. FREE AIR (broken hose). Head of a deer (shorn from her) rest. Plugs of mudflesh. Her mangled gaze poked with sticks. Boys after oily night. Crows (handsome violators). Lust her (scattered) gravities. Headlight's (coming vertical) lifting splitting trees. Budtips (starry black nets). A going of (migratory distortion). Of charcoal rubies. Birds (burning ink) are broken rubies. Beetling (hard sinking) west.

ACCIDENT OF ERROR KING

Tonight's moon's
palm-bed color of yellow ghost
    seabirds elsewhere
        feeding (simple theft)
in lead and milk mist (confusing
    its location) over
        lake's a stun of sweet
mercuries falling lands losing chin
    to rain to pine needles
    ground to spice on
(I am walking) oceanside path's
    pink slabstones massed
        rootbacks (blackslicks)
(accident of snaking) comes a small
    can of (sun's making
        leaves) making errors of
shadow and slips and paws (up-
    ended moons) wristing
    white birches come gulls
(winged indifference) to each grass
    a king (lake's blind)
    silverleapt dimples a love-
jump for a daisy's bee (its one
    daisy) gives its face
        sun (takes)

Golf Course Living At Its Best; Register Here For A Free Glamour Portrait; Vending Cafe; Twenty Thousand Dollar Drive; Vacuum Towel Fragrance; $AV-A-BUK Venetian Blinds; Assorted Upright Foliage, $4.99; Destination: Excellence; He Soaked His Toes In His Wife's Crockpot; Wholesale Carnival Goods; Elevator Emergency Response Unit; Señorita Burrito; Hot Dog In A Turtleneck; Frozen Fish Shapes; Parisian Peel, $149.99; Part-Time Phlebotomist; Night Shift Operator Oral-B Domestic; Animal Trainer; Seven Cities Sod; Wak 'N' Yak House Of Hair; Fractures, Sprains, And Dislocations; Lovers, All Unfaithful; University Of The South Pole; University of the Hobo; Señor $1 Store; Never Not A Sale.

Last Living Splits Familiar Thuds Yelping Oak

A skeleton descends a staircase.
Click clack click clack. This was her house. A collision
          of wintering ribs licked with wind and ice
disconcerts dogwoods, uplawn, seeded
too close. She begins a poem:
          Black honey in a womb
(there is no middle).

It ends.

Night tricks dream from bed to bed.
          Day's a seizure of daisies.
Clouds crumble their hems. A scenic eruption comes yelping in trickles.
          A radio confirms:
          A day has turned up missing slipped between a pair of nights.

A week last month is interrogated.

She locates sleep, sitting up, in a porch swing. Arms of day assemble
          from night's sunk bloom tossed to a chairback.
Dreams are black thuds in jars, unlabeled, sold three for a nickel, ago.
          She awakens, *click clack click clack,* and of split throatings
of a lane'd oak asks:

Was there a road here once?

And waits. In day's acid wink she waits until these last bones living,
          this deafening dreaming, are not.
A pocket knife found in the sideboard is a familiar shape
in her hand of sticks.
          She carves into a kneecap a name, any, recalled.

LIMB YARD FREED OF VOICY HAT BLACK SCISSORING

Under evening's
pigmentary wash
      horizon's tangerine pearlglove
brings night's
      coming backthroat—
      (a stung stain)
      loosing
limb yards
      (creaky wands)
      chatterhung
(sat with)
      hatblack birds
      (seedbloats)
(going madly) scissoring day's last
      lowersome lake
(stars are pins)
      dimwinked
      (or stingholes)
into sky's open stitch
      accentuals
lifting (filefly) to
      land missing
whereverwhere
      (voicy messes)
(flown disborn)
      gone
      lovely

III

Dreamweek in Luxury Jars
I Yell in Candy Thrown War

GALWAY KINNELL is my chauffeur.
He lets me sit up front.
He says: *You know what you always say!*
I have no idea what I always say, pretending otherwise.

GIANT SAMURAI at a luxury house vacuuming rigorously.
I find a wad of door keys in the pool drain.
Coming to sun is a race of squirrels with beautiful human faces.

AN OLD HOTEL and I ride the lousy bones of its antique elevator.
Buttons pushed with stubborn clicks.
Taken to floors not sequentially numbered.

BOX CARS of a train are giant Kleenex boxes.
Tissues fume from open tops.

A CALICO CAT is talked out of suicide.
This is my skill.
I have driven far to be with a room of people I don't know.
Among them I gain the reputation of healer of talking cats.

AS A DELI WORKER I have questionable success.
Questionable success in the construction of a ham sandwich.
The owner sells cigarettes to young girls.
The lips of young girls swum in angry cranberries.

CHRISTINE, a childhood friend, is awarded a Fulbright for camping.

BILL CLINTON is on crutches, a leg amputated below the knee.
He runs a foot-race around a track behind the White House.
I yell from the sidelines: *Take the inside lane! Save it for the last hundred yards!*
He loses.

DRESSER DRAWERS of sea water.
Palms stained blue.
Coming back to life in the arms of his master is a mummified dog.
A mummified dog singing Christmas carols.

73

A WOMAN pulls a pair of brussel sprouts from her pants.
She throws the brussels sprouts from the car.
We speed.
Wide and chuckling green faces of brussels sprouts keep apace.

I STAND on the tracks, a hand out for help.
A train comes.
A man in an overcoat too small stands awkward on a hilltop.
He will not extend a hand to help.
He is afraid of falling.

BACKYARDS of identical suburban homes.
A man on a sit-down mower gives a ride to a scarecrow in his lap.
The man enjoys the ride much more than the scarecrow.

WE ARE AT WAR.
It is unclear who 'we' are.
The opponent: a Chinese restaurant and the family that owns it.
We advance toward the buffet, red vinyl booths smoldering.
Three Chinese men throw handfuls of things like orangy pebbles into my lap.
I dive fearing bombs but it is candy, hard candy.
The men approach, smiles blooming in charcoal crescents.

NEW TEETH CONSPIRE HIS DEAD SEX COILED

In a bed not her own.
A dream of his dead sex.
Moon's bald lid tongues.
Bricks head to foot back to belly.
Walling man across a courtyard ironing.
2 a.m. again.
In a bed not her own a dream of his.
Across a country.
Anemic straps of light gentling bowls of subway seats.
Under clouds of new teeth.
In a bed not her own a dream to a wall in a box.
A man living on the steps of a public library.
His daily lecture: *I never met a toy not part of a conspiracy!*
Above her.
In a bed not her own.
A family of four in a room for one.
Up at 5 a.m.
Water plows.
A dream and in it a flower shop.
Toe joints snap to dresser to closet to shower to kitchen.
And out.
Before light.
In a bed not her a dream of his dead sex in a room for one.
A dream coiled to a wall in a long white box.
A long white box from the flower shop.

HOAGIE DAY'S BIGGEST TITS UNSPEAKING MURDER

SETTING #1
School cafeteria. 5th grade. Hoagie Day. A Friday.

INCITING INCIDENT
A note, slid onto your tray: *I'm gonna fuck you up.* Playground. Recess.

AUTHOR OF THE ABOVE
Gwen Roberts: biggest tits in the 5th grade.

SETTING #2
Playground. A series of slaps to the head. You retort with a flail. All air.

REACTION
A call from the pay phone by the faculty lounge: *I am being assassinated.*

INTERMISSION
You wait on the curb where the buses idle.

DENOUEMENT
Blue Nova pulls up containing your mother and her pink orb of foam curlers.

HOME
You refuse to return to school. For three days. You are called into The Office.

UNLIKELY OUTCOME
A reprimand from the vice-principal. You are a truant.

WITNESS
Face of Jimmy Carter and his yellow skyscraper teeth above a file cabinet.

RESULT
You consider giving up all forms of communication. This includes speech.

SECONDARY RESULT
Talk therapy with Dr. Kaplan. He makes you play with some clay.

PARALLEL ACTION
Your mother returns a set of napkin rings.

PROGRESS
You do not speak for seven sessions.

PRIMARY RESULT
Dr. Kaplan tries the angry technique.

RESULT
Bits of egg salad rocket from his confusion of teeth and land on your poncho.

HEIGHTENED ACTION
He yells. *Say something goddammit!*

NEXT TO FINAL ACTION
You flee into the waiting room.

EXTERIOR CONFLICT
Gnawing the carpet is the next patient: a boy who swallows office supplies.

TERTIARY ACTION
Over him you trip into a fishbowl.

TERTIARY RESULT
Murder: a pair of goldfish.

AFTERSTORY
Speaking confirmed forever unnecessary.

Invented was the Easter Bunny by the Pennsylvania Dutch.
The summer of the haircut.
Refusing to join the swim team for breasts not yet.
For unheated was the spring-fed community pool.
The summer we were thought Dutch.
But not Dutch.
Pennsylvanian.
So to the Liberty Bell.
Since Philadelphian.
Five class trips a year.
All the bus rides.
A classmate vomits potholes of Lebanon bologna on the Homeroom Mother.
Not Mrs. Shoemaker.
Shoemaker: a popular Pennsylvania Dutch name.
Mrs. Shoemaker and her one long tooth for 59 years in one room.
A front room rented for $34 a month from Grandma Jesse.
In central Pennsylvania.
New Bloomfield, Pennsylvania.
Her daily anarchy: dancing shoeless on a balcony its posts rotted.
And a trip to Intercourse, Pennsylvania.
Kountry Kitchen Buffet.
Since we are Pennsylvanian.
As not yet were the Amish on rollerblades or cocaine.
As it is the sixth grade milk is spooned into water glasses.
This makes mushroom clouds.
As it is the sixth grade mashed potatoes deposit into milk.
Flung from spoons: peas.
And one dollar each to spend on Pennsylvania Dutch Rainbow Taffy.
Or a pink plastic backscratcher printed with INTERCOURSE, PA, in gold.
And he takes the dollar.
The man with the wire wool beard obesing his chin.
We are in dresses and kneesocks and our good shoes.
Since it was then.
Home we sing.
A Man Named Jed in the unbuttoned dark.
Turnpike exit: King of Prussia and on it: The Leon Spinks Motel.

For when Leon Spinks fought that one time and won.
And we sing.
A man named Jed a poor mountaineer barely kept his family fed and then one day.
Over seats we pass it and take turns scratching backs.
The official souvenir Pennsylvania Dutch plastic pink backscratcher.
INTERCOURSE, PA, stamped in gold passed from back to back.
Backseat: it's the class couple since fourth grade.
Her brows are moist pebbles.
Their heads profile.
Then one day he was shootin' at some crude.
In faltering rose glow his hand maps her flat breast.
A hand working in mechanical circles.

Stars soon to be fleeced of hearing.
For it is $40 up stairs littered with Q-Tips and Friskies.
Your Aura by Miss Laura asks if she may smoke and smokes anyway.
And for $200 more, while I am away, she will clean my aura.
No, honey, I clean it while you are at home.
Just leave the money.
It'll take only a week and mine needs it.
A lot of work.
Another dozen candles lit.
Arms flap to dispel me.
In this cubicle of cardboard, we tilt.

And for free I offer to recite my three favorite obituaries:

   1). The Cue Card King
   2). The Inventor of Melba Toast
   3). The Inventor of the Hungry Man TV Dinner

Offer refused.
Waiting room is the dining room.
Black banana skins threaded through with coat hanger wire
   over a doorway.
Out slinks a cat of course black: an eye sucked shut as if glued.
On both of mine.
His one hard moon.

TRAVELOGUE #909-V: NEATLY SMOKING UP HER GOING

Shod with dross, his,
    since telophase
    she crouches on her tinderbox—
tracer bullets
    smoking yellow up her greened
spine de-bussing her self-implanted
timing chain that knows only
    going: her t-squared
    plans of cloroxed past
    with big dumb feet over
tattooed
bodysuit
    leaves no mark

Man with Blue Guitar saves girl baby from the Oncoming X.
Then checks out baby's mother's ass.
He moves his form.
His form does not move him.
His social impossibility!
He may say: *I am! Let me!*
Not in saying, but in how his legs walk him.
For his legs walk him!
His legs!
Composing headrhymes of dimes and sometimes crime.
Since he's seen it.
Now she.
For he is!
Art is!
She.
Paint—what color.
A lime-drop shoulder.
Fingertips droop pearl.
Of flat blue tubes—a nose.
For a wrist strung—a white nose!
But perhaps longer.
Sea-eroded eye holes.
A black fence, away from here.
Two browns: one darkled blue stiffs an icy beard.
And the tip of!
A bear's nose!
A glowing skate of neck and a tree's black thumb.
Whitened, a wrist breaking.
Gently strumming tapers.
Flickered wicks.
For he strums.
Away from falling.

BLACK HAT ON 1952 FORTUNATELY YELLOW CHAIR

I came from the desert born up from sand fully clothed which was fortunate for no money was born into my pockets. I was dressed as a man which was fortunate for I wouldn't have known I was not otherwise. It was a loose-fitting jacket with notch lapels the color of tobacco without cuffs which was fortunate. For I prefer informality and cuffs are about those who prefer tea or cigars. In my mouth I was born with no cigar for babies born as men have no need of them. Fortunately, I was born enhatted or hattened or hatable or hatly or with hat, for elsewise I would not have known what my head was for. For I was born grown but not yet experienced in mind or sense. This is also true of the setting into which I was born, for look around—it is a world shy of all possible colors, perhaps so, to relieve landscape of itself. For clouds and a dove and a rock are cartooned black and filled with white as are the posts and styles of the ladderback chair (upon which I was arrived) that is out of perspective, not of course to me but from five or six paces down front and away. See that situated near my birthchair is a thriving succulent horned and green with black shadings and a toothsome sideways mouth nesting charcoal teeth singing at full throat, if it could sing. Ready to fly is a dove, with, for an eye, a watermelon seed tipped on its behind not singing for she has no line in the proper place to open her beak. Wings aflung, she regards my disregarded perspective at what would be, if I would have remained, my neck. Above, cut out and affixed to flat cobalt for sky are three adhesed lumps of misshapen bone filled here and there with ashy smudges the size of bruises. Below lies a grasping succulent with taloned points reaching in a curl at precisely where my ankles were born, which was fortunate, for I would not have known what my ankles were for, but to receive the tickling. Unfortunate are the horns of green too close to my hat which incurred a stab to my hip, but was fortunate in the end, for elsewise, I would not have known I possessed a hip. What is here then, in place of myself is my hat, left to the criss-crossing flat sticks of black over yellow that informed me that here is a seat of a chair, for how would I know what sitting was for, except that it precedes rising, if one rises at all. Rising I did, careful to leave no footprints, which wasn't so hard, for I had none, taking not my hat nor my jacket nor my chair though my chair's equal proportions of black and white appealed to my eye's sense of here and not here. See, I am who has travelled over the sooty line that rambles downwest that tells sand from heavylidded blue from muscular snouts of green-risen succulents born to support a dove not singing. For I am not so beautiful as the scene I have left you though I could have left it a bit more tidy, for I left those few lines to lie in the sand that are composed like this: '52 F. LÉGER' though I know not what it means, though it may be an ancient alphabet or an accident of burnt sticks and I thought it best not to kick sand over it, as I was leaving under a sky removed of sun, born into a desert with no need of sun. For a sun is naturally bossy and pushes shadows into hard leans at the beginnings and ends of days, jostling days into continual risings and leavings, which I have no part in. This, I think, is most fortunate.

OPEN LETTER TO MR. FERNAND LÉGER, WITH RESPONSE

What, Mr. Fernand Léger: Am I to make of your ill-legged chair with hat and jacket and man-eating plants placed impossibly in a desert? Mr. Léger, I have been to the desert. In daylight I have seen the sun (a grand omission in your *Black Hat on a Yellow Chair*). And in the desert, in sky, is always sun, which may of course be missing from your art, but missing are the effects of her. And this is a crime. A world minus shadow is one less the complexity that makes it. And who has left his hat? And jacket? Art is life and art missing a subject is minus life. Has the owner of the hat and jacket strolled up and over that skating black line that you take for horizon? Horizons are anything if horizontal, for one. And the desert is to be respected if but for the danger if it. Are you for life or its opposite? Yes, Mr. Léger, I have been to the desert and in the desert, a hat is better left on one's head than on one's seat.
　　—*Mr. George Catlin, portrait artist, Gallery Rear, Iowa Museum of Art*

Mr. Catlin, what I see: Is that I paint what I see and you are welcome to paint what you see. You see men and woman unafraid to perhaps sit on rocks or pose in desert. I see that you see a man by the name of Mad Buffalo with hair ornamented with a great many silver brooches that extends quite down to the knees. I see that you see he has eyes hot lit and red-rimmed and black hair to the waist dipped in red to the line of his chin, lightning zigs of red on his chest, red finger-paint encircling each nipple. I see that you see Midday Sun, a woman in white sheepskin to her ankles and a necklace of mink heads and plumes of porcupine quills and flaming red balls for cheeks. I see that you see a black-painted handprint over the mouth of a man seated on a rock and his ears more made of earrings than ear. I see that you see a hunter and prey dying heaped on one another of red wounds in red ice and snow. I see you have made object of your subject. I have made subject of object. I see what I see and I see, Mr. Catlin, what you see.
　　—*Translated from the French by Val Brill, Day Guard, Iowa Museum of Art*

85

GREETINGS WORDS BECAUSE I AM USING AMERICA

Mrs. Terry Like
1 Glorious Way
Singing Hive, FL 82234

Mr. Rodney Wu, Director Word Selection and Placement
GO AMERICAN Greeting Card Company
Department AA-211: Love, Death, Pet's Birthdays
56000-A Plus Way, Lucky, KS   00216

Dear Mr. Wu,

Greetings from America! This is in response to your open call for
'Word Selection and Placement Operators' in the Sunday supplement
of the *Sun Tower Times*. Enclosed are three samples. My background is
that I am an American and have been using words since, roughly, age three.

LOVE
OUTSIDE: Artist's rendering of a Wal-Mart, its roof in flames.
INSIDE: *For Only You, This Is What, I'd Do I'd Do*

SYMPATHY
OUTSIDE: Artist's rendering of the Rockettes kicking over tombstones.
INSIDE: *Love is For Those Living: Death For Those—Not*

PET BIRTHDAY
OUTSIDE: Rendering of a dog on a hospital gurney, an IV in its leg.
INSIDE: *Chocolate makes Doggies sick; celebrate with beef sticks.*

Thank you for your time and consideration,

Mrs. Terry Like

So Wot Ar Wordz Makeing Fansy O Literally!

So Wot ar words-
worth?
    O i'ts not lik withe out it them, Im'e goi'nto thurz to deth!—
    I evun hear'd too muche-e wurds makeing fansy flower'y
blumes out yor pen
    can obsorb yer brain, exvaporate it, make it disupire, go
eggstinkt!
    O that w-
ool'd be teribal.

    See b'ecouse th mor wir-d's you ar you-seing th mor worsier
becums yor beeng abell to remumber! O litteralliey!
    Damadge is don!
    (An th'at meens smallier performin-
ts bu-twene yer earsz)

    A cotastrafee!
    An so what-'f yo wantto mak monnnye at it—at makein-g
wordz? Do'nt mak me H-a!
    O it-ell coste you'e!
    Yull'e gett a humpp'ed back and mumbb'le unsit'ly noiz-es an
gett l'ooke'd at sidey-ey'ed.
    An wotta'bout or erthly aire? Th'at we breath-e?

Wrd's hav-to go sommwayre and gue'ss wheyere? Repaci'ng'th ocksagen
riht form the aire with smudjes of ink'y thawgh'ts—
    O itz a mess-ey mettli'ng with-e oour earz our ey'es! Wee neede
those'e!
    Cosing helth to expore!
    Wot ar words-

thenbut: clatter'ng blethr-ng blustrrin'g an bedlamb!
    An with to-o much-ey airbourne wordz grduaelly, avenchely
and probally
    peeoeple's lungz ar gointo exsplode. Dockters don need-e to've
studd-ye'd th scientz of it!

O do'nt actsept it!
    Butt the'n trulyeye I one daye settley'ed withe a longe
empurlped horisz'n an
thoultht thys:

        Wurdes are s'o in-icspensive!
        An Frie!
        Free'as aire!
(Iff allyou wantto do'iz playe monkeey withemme).
        Then'ne lettthm go free'e!
(An in mye opeinyun thatze th'betterbest waye,
        sinse and becausse in th'e nd, so

        Wot arew-
wordsweirth?)
(thinke onthiese starss: * * *)
        O okaye thinkgin's over.

So in conclusit, wemay-ahswell breath'them.

        O!

Wordd'sz to 'breath-e!
        Fre-e: for ever onne culde hav iether m-
any or so-manee or too-o manny an still-e thair'se enoph!
        An enoph is exspeshully goo'd.

No onne lift out!
        Consiter it!

        O! O! *O!*

A sky looms loosely cindered—
    another season
        sun lips low
        habitable
a pond mown to black mirror
a pair of sweet weeds
        bathing in the color of pond
a hand in her hair's known dark
    free of twist
        grass's pale brilliance
breasts iridesce lime and burgundy musics
eyes sing stories
    they believe
        feet of young crows
a sulfured profile collects
    risen color of grasses
    born of guitars
        strung with miniature violets—
a fourth nude
    her knees
    identical roses
speaking
    in fire knots

Down by the ankles of the Holy See : I ker-chink a dime into the < ! > machine and turn the: *ker-chong-g-g* crank. Out pops a photograph of a Ravine. I run to it. A hundred miles. Dive in, wonder, for how I came to be: in this photograph of a ravine for a hundred years. So. Up shows the Devil [in a devil costume]. He yells down into my up-looking face, *You're way off, lady. Three ravines to the right.* I see no more ravines to the right or right. So. What is there but to:

Down by the ankles of the Holy See : I ker-chink a dime into the < ! > machine and turn the: *ker-chong-g-g* crank. Out pops a photograph of a Man I forgot to. I dive into it, wonder for years at how these children are not. So. Up shows: Epictetus [in an Ancient Greek philosopher costume]. He yells into my down-looking face: *Freedom? Destroy What You Desire!* I thought I had thought I had flung. All that. Across my country tis of this gets me. So thinking:

Down by the ankles of the Holy See : I ker-chink a dime into the < ! > machine and turn the: *ker-chong-g-g* crank. Out pops a photograph of an eye. Minus its ocean. I dive into it for years. I ask why I like it here. A lot. Plenty of swimming. So. Up shows: Mason less Dixon [in splashy organdy velvet knickers]. I am the first to yell, *I wish you'd stayed home.* (I didn't want to be. Discovered). I am ignored. Busy as he is with his sextant. Too full with horizon to hear. So:

Down by the ankles of the Holy See : I ker-chink a dime into the < ! > machine and turn the: *ker-chong-g-g* crank. Out pops a photograph of walking. I dive. Woven beyond light. For years I wonder of why but not of my wandering. So. Up shows Rousseau [dressed like a French philosopher whose invective seeded Revolution] yelling (in translation): *The Inconceivable Author Of Nature Is Not So.* So this: Being. I Yawn. Thinking so:

Down by the ankles of the Holy See : I ker-chink a dime into the < ! > machine and turn the: *ker-chong-g-g* crank. Out pops a photograph of The End. I dive in and think of when I will not: hold, draw, write, spit, injure, love, run to from to. When. On my lap, watered light. My hands of Wheels with Eyes. I yell: *I.* But Up shows (spoiler): My body [Dressed in a bodysuit]: My forehead, says, *I am too bodied not to.* I am too here. *To hear.* (Hear a sigh).

July.

Heat on (high) dash and floor (phouuuuuuuu).
(Insane) man (she) is married (to) (for) now is.
Driving (he carols) *dinkle dinkle doo* (dinkley dinkley doo):
Methinks, so I do.

Pull over:
        ((pulled (over) for weaving (*weaving he is*))
by Officer (small coin + accidental fall) = Sergeant Pennyslip.
(((((((((She is (in) the (death) seat.))))))))))
        Unbuckled.
But if so (buckled) so (what)?:

For it's *dinkle dinkle doo* (dinkley dinkley doo).
        Achoo (or in French, *achoo*).
But so. Interior:
        Locks (automatic).
        Windows (up).
        Sealed (in).

Jersey Turnpike exits (closed): 8A and 11.
Rest (stops) open:
        Molly Pitcher.
        Walt Whitman.
        Tiffany Trump (future).

Fooey fooey foo (fooey fooey foo).
        You (you).
        Her (body) (shorts) (out).
        Thanking))))))(overly)(((((the toll man.
Again asks)))she((((him):
        Is it again, yet?

I.
I have a bit of a headache say the movie subtitles.
Me too, from the couch of Famous People in Odd Settings.

II.
But not yet.
This is the watching of a girl watching herself in the coffeehouse mirror
watched by a boy fatigued but polite-alert to girl talking in pogo sticks
of single-stall bathrooms or
if he can guess where the extra frozen french fries are stored since
it's all about her job at Deli Mart.

III.
Or yet.
It is Our Circuit Trainer.
He introduces himself with credentials:
I trained out of Des Moines.
We dodge a few cones. Jump rope. Boxer shuffle. Sprint, bad knees
clicking, line-to-painted line and twenty minutes too soon it's over since
he hadn't planned the timing. He's *getting used to the new gym.*

IV.
Tonight only.
ACT I: George Clooney in a sealed cardboard box, painted black, center stage.
ACT II: Lemonade lighting. Violins tuning, not playing, for an hour.
ACT III: A collapse to full black and the George Clooney box collapses.
And inside there is no George Clooney.
AND CURTAIN.

V.
EXTERIOR: It is America.
NOW: She drives past the Sinclair service station dinosaur
up to its kindergarten green, clavicled in snow.
LATER: Casino parking and recreational homes with three for $10
folding chairs bungee-corded to bumpers and signs
crafted from wood-burning kits in garages across the fruited:
Hello We Are the Wilmers. Or Wigmores. Or. Or.

VI.

INTERIOR: Nickel Slots.

FUTURE: His wife remembers not to leave herself in the ladies' room.
For it is up through the broken elbows of corn
to Menard's Home Center he wants to go.
With his winnings. Buckets of nickels. Five of them.
On sale as advertised: *Beautiful Artificial Authentic Looking Trees.*

It Takes Two of Them and So No Flying into It

Christmas is opened.
Missing by noon is one of two frogs.
And the greasy head of ham appears on the buffet.
And the polished butts of miniature carrots.
Ant farm minus ants.
Again the nephew asks: *When will the ant farm ants be arriving?*
(Under separate cover from the factory.)
One light frizzes out on the Christmas tree.
And so all the lights frizz out on the Christmas tree.

There is no lightning on Venus.
And of the quartz rock the width of a hair found in Australia?
Containing molecules of oxygen.
Water predates fire.

So this is the beginning.
No flaming things.
No cloud-to-cloud lightning.
And so no flying.
Into it.

Escaped:
Texas men who *Hid In Plain Sight Frequenting Coffee Shops And Night Clubs.*
They flew into it by walking!

That it takes three of them to caulk the door frame across the street.
All day it's this.

This impediment of sight.

Natural Man exercises American Pockets of earlier vocabularies.
Drug whole from Homer and Hercules and Crocodile Dundee.
(Same thing.)
To K-Mart, Aisle 8: Comes Natural Man. Charioteer!
To sales on socks on saltines on and on.
Customers of Age Uncertain are knocked to asses.
For he bounds!
Natural Man! To Pets and Fish.
To Patio and Barbeque. To flay a gerbil! To roast it.
Gadzooks!
And to What Shiny Spoils! Costume Jewelry! Fine leather sacks!
One across his chest.
Quickly clasped to keep Wind Home from leaping free.
Comes galumphing: Bob (Just Bob): Branch Manager.
Nine years of faithful service on a dial-less phone he.
Security! Security!
To Home Furnishings Natural Man charioteers.
To admire metal-stapled joinery of particle board bed set.
But where lie the beautiful wives? His?
Of Eight-Items-Or-Less's Check-out girl, he asks.
He brings her to believe!
She has song! So she sings.
Natural Man's eyes on her mouth's cheap pink.
On her.
He wills her.
Until!
Her Taller Throat sees into his Only Ghost.
And for singing she screams.
And leaps Natural Man. Aft of exit.
Detectors WAH-WAH-WAHing.
Comes security to lock down.
To automatic sliding doors Natural Man bounds.
With fists he pounds!
He pounds the magic from.

Not without A You! Twin-other. It's all about the You! Of You! The You of me! Dreams of walking, matched strides. On glass clouds. Hips pinned. Or somewhere up high! Usually, You are a little taller. Or it's a walk in a city, where You now live with the woman called Your wife. But that's only one You. One of the You's! There are other You's. Pockets full! I stay up late. Lug the You's around. A dream: We play, though grown! In our socks. A game of spy. A woman fills a suitcase on a bed with Leaving-Things. We huddle and through a hole in the floor, watch! You and the You of me. I watch Your profile watching, a point not moving from its pin. It's law but it's not written. Nor is it planetary! For there is no revolving! It's like this: A boy in a car. It's a new-old car. His first. Backing from the drive, adjusting himself in the rear-view mirror. A night ahead! A sun of years above! And she watching burns her own fire because she is born to burn her own. His rounds of shoulders warmed from behind. Face burning with leap he leaps her flame. To different kinds of travelling. Satellite sighted. It's The You of You, moving. The Autobiography! All You. All of You.

EARLY LOGIC CONFUSES RUIN ON BUTTER TATTOO

PROOF 1: $a + (b1) - c = y$

IF **a**:	First Grade. You like to read. Abraham Lincoln liked to read.
+ **b1**	You write in your best big block letters, keeping in the lines: LINCOLN LIKED TO READ BY A CANDLE.
- **c**:	*Liked it?* huffs teacher Mrs. Stahl. *Dim light hurt his eyes!*

THEN: **A CONFUSED EARLY LOGIC**

PROOF 2: $a - (b1) + c - (b2) - (d1) = y^2$

IF **a**:	You are 11. On your bike. Straddling the bar, not the seat.
- **b1**	There is no pillow secured over said bar.
+ **c**	Neighbor boys are out front—
- **b2**	—within earshot.
- **d1**:	Your mother's mouth from kitchen window: *You are going to ruin your vagina!*

THEN: **AN EARLY HUMILIATION**

PROOF 3: $a + b - (c1) - (c2) + d - (c3) - d - d = y^3$

IF **a**:	You are single. Anywhere from 18–88.
+ **b**:	In five minutes he will arrive. A second date.
- **c1**:	He is a dog catcher-trainee.
- **c2**:	Up for promotion twice— —passed over for smuggling lost animals (into air-conditioned matinees).
+ **d**:	He calls from the car. Boasts of a new tattoo:
- **c3**:	a pair of actual-sized pats of melting butter—
- **d**:	—on his left ass cheek.
- **d**:	You hide under the piano, lights out, until he quits knocking.

THEN: **AN EARLY NIGHT**

FIVE-KU ON SOONER HOLEY HEAVEN

ME-KU
After all the you's
          the honeymoon I alone
took was, by far, best.

PLAY-KU
Act I: Exit All.
          Act II: (off-stage) A Shot! *Nooo-o-o-o!*
Act III: Moon falls. *Klunk.*

BROKE-KU
Ice Slip, Traction None—
          Tires Bald, Money None—Holey
Pockets: Sooner Heav'n.

OBFUS-KU
So! When if? In of—
          Comes then! This so: what (not). Ha!
Linger now. Away!

REMINDER-KU
Remember that once
          you halved me and halved me and
halved me and halved m—?

MOVING MAKES RED CANCELLING OPPOSITE HORIZON

A blow to the head. Blood. Drama. A ride in the back of a police car.
Red light performing the dogma of circular motion though if in
a pocket mirror reversed. As I am 10 we end in ice cream and
the extreme condition at the heart of a star stealing mass.
I reflect on reverse and that you work equally well backward
and forward. Then you are an act of recession. From this
I follow your collides. As you are symmetrical you are difficult
to grasp. As I am in kneesocks I carry that mathematical point
of singularity in an open bucket not yet a universe. This is long
after you learn to spell Jesus with not a "g." Moving freely in
the heat. Order at high temperatures is why her cheeks redden
when obsessed with the perfectibility of her apartment. Pointing
at random after I return to precisely zero. Again comes
the problem of an opposite horizon. This hundred doublings
of anything of size to macroscopic: cancelled precisely at the
intersections of Rt. 6IA and Black Top Road. Not born but bled.
Eleven stitches are X's a pirate makes for treasure not yet buried
on a brow. Above this eye.

FOR YOU WERE BORN McASIAN BLUE
BUTTERING INVISIBLE CLANS

Arrives. A mailbox of bathing suits with girls in them. A boy's blurred
　　　smile kicking sand. Eating the beautiful riddles, I leave you
　　　lightly. For how else? Upon waking, the desire to burn my
　　　juvenalia. There is nothing left. My borders move, alone.
　　　Canada: A man there, with an accident to the head, and a career
　　　from it. America: A boy, special, his job at Goodwill, his blue
　　　smock, out from behind Summer Pants, tells me: *Coats are there.*
　　　I follow his lemon pink finger, my hair on end, for I was looking
　　　for coats, specifically, yet had not yet asked. What's true:
　　　Perfection costs $5. I wear it.

McAsian I say: That you are Korean, wear the kilt of my clan and
　　　McInize your name? Please do, for I am born the white devil,
　　　though not binary, but blue. And this is what I can not say: I
　　　love you, McAsian, please make vaudeville in the kilt of my
　　　clan: Raped again, by no one! I quit words, for pictures. ENTER
　　　SCREEN LEFT: Nose tip of the name God, for many seconds
　　　moving, a violet carrot, sawing raw what's left of horizon.
　　　Following his nose, a face. CLOSE ON: Invisible jesus
　　　of no color, the color of plasma, a profile, in hard stain.

Will be a folk art featured in theme villages with pluses and minuses you can't give away! And butter mints in gold foil, complimentary, printed with dusty equations perhaps four for a dollar or perhaps for free will be The Genius, his second coming in second, who runs the Fifth Avenue Mile yelling *The sun is on fire! The sun is one fire.* To her! We sing for happy and lost and recovery will be our First Real War finished before begun as around will be no detail to configure with. For here we will be at One Address, One Driveway that wraps the equator, One Giant mailbox the size of Nevada plus a snib of Idaho. But no longer Nevada! Or necessary mailings. Nor secrets with necessity licked. Nor the defines of line. For A will not predate C and Y no longer is strung to nearly. The end. And so, no longer will maps. Nor anything with lines nor border crossings and triggermen in fatigues and mustaches also dusty from unrotated crops across barbed wire fingers inked red with stampings of official papers checking identities unknown to going. For this: To the One-shirted raiser of baby lettuces in what was another hemisphere will be known the successful thief des bicyclettes in what was this hemisphere to whom will be known the collector of decorative buttons sticky with Sobo glue making paper plate faces not meant for sale. On a kitchen table. Slicked with what went of suns she thrills to find the perfect eye: A honey sung sepia glued on and it is her eye for she will know not—remembering.

TRAVELOGUE #3-V: FAILURE OF PARADISE UNENDING

Again.
He sews those fancy buttons onto her holocaust. Meanwhile.
Where to shop?
> The 99¢ store?
> The 88¢ store?
> In a river laryngitic.

Light blotty through leaf.

After the dog:
> She bet it all on the lake.
> Option: Sell a lung.

See my hands?
Over my ears?

To make it up to him:
She looks all over for one of those gizmos that make applesauce:

> A day hand-grinding spices.
> A night tossing windows.

What's whispered into the ear of the carcass is met with applause.
> Across our genital sprawl.

Into: she exits.
> At Hot Song.

AFTER OCTOBER OF ANOTHER TIME AND BOB INTO

A horizon jeweling tin. So comes the title for her book BOB! We celebrate: to Truck On 'N. And it's half price on Golden Deliciouses raised at BOB's (different BOB's) Golden Delicious farm. Suffer not from lonenesse says OLD POET when sun blinds and heroes think cheated. Leave earthly understanding unshoed, of sticky faith, says OLD PHILOSOPHER since which Duchamp squared the circle. With a four-footed stool born. In a century just previous you. Know this, and that small towns are left bereft after major films are filmed there. Horizon's red weight swims chaste. And out comes a book of poems entitled BOB! every poem entitled 'BOB' for reasons known only to her and to this said BOB for whom she begins work on a claymation of Mr. Alighieri's *Inferno*. For says OLD POET (New old POET): *We come from where we desire to return* and how not easy to hang those clay figures by their little ankles poked through with steel wire! Heads to shoulders in boiling sludge. Cries of strange trees. Knowing only now and not the question of where lives specifically BOB. South Pasadena. Not a farmer but a master of knives. On children. His hands gifted with the miniature precision of raindrops. In a future waits a book and lesson #4: POISE. Dogs trot neighborhoods with books entitled BOB! on blocky heads searching for the lovelinesse (spells OLD POET) (same old poet) within. Comes one to ask: Is it lovelie that she requests BOB's scalpels hung? For together now at the end of it having lived all of it—apart, but at this end he will remove his shirt to pluck from her chin a few old lady hairs and it is an act of love though the acts are missing and when sun dreams of cooling her cheek's cradle she will come to, to cooling.